Poetry from the Potting Shed

By Jack Kerr

CLASSIFICATION: POETRY

Second Edition published in Great Britain in 2016 by Sarah E Brace

ISBN-13: 978-1511468091

Photo Credits:
Sarah Brace (Cover)
Kieran Kerr (Back cover)

To Gerda my soulmate and wife of 59 years and our three lovely children:
Karl and his fiancée Sally, Daniel and his wife Marie, mother of our grandsons
Kieran and Christopher, and Sarah with partner Phil.
Also my 'little sister' Jill.

Contents

"A Full Life's Work Before Us Laid"

Queen of Spades

Green fingered, Gerda in her garden stands,
Glittering grey eyes, gardener's hands.
Nature's daughter, mother of the soil
Queen of Spades, her kingdom royal.

Season by season her year proceeds
Giving the soil what soe'er it needs,
Potash, compost, manure or lime
Each to each at its allotted time.

Forking, digging, sowing seeds,
Raking, pruning, pulling weeds,
Gerda moves with nature's rhythm
Rotates her beds and what thrives in them.

Now the season of autumnal damp,
A hole she digs to form a clamp.
Lines it well with good clean straw,
Winterlong safe, cosy root crop store.

And after glorious summer it does attest
An extra bountiful fruitful harvest.
In trays of reds, greens, yellows and dapples,
Gerda's spartan, bramley and sunset apples.

Her sparkling eyes like diamonds shine,
Her blessed realm entwined with mine.
A full life's work before us laid
With heartfelt love her tribute paid
In beauty crafted with a spade.

A Bowl of Cherries

Strawberries are sweet – you must agree
Blackberries brimming with vitamin C.
Raspberries so packed full of flavour,
Cranberries tart, but that apart,
Can our nether organs favour!
Gooseberries' delicious, delectable tang,
Oft their praises have we sang.
Then the peerless blueberry –
Perfect prince of all the berries.
Though my favourite fruit is not a berry,
But the rich, ruby-red and heavenly cherry
And you my love, my bowl of cherries.

GM

I saw a leek, post GM
With a rose on top and a thick red stem.
And a potato genetically modified
Growing, yet sizzling, already fried.
See the throbbing new black currant,
Vitamin C with electric current.
Please don't touch, the shocks are real,
Morphed with genes from electric eel.
Rows of peas and rows of beans
And some, a sort of 'in-betweens'
And Brussels sprouts and rhubarb sticks
Performing playful party tricks.
Turnips and swedes, deep rooted brassicas
Now sport genes that cure sciaticas,
Chew some raw, rub some on and, oh, I say
That awful pain just went away.
Perhaps when summer days drowse long
You'll hear tomatoes sing a song,
While Pentland Javelins cleave the air
And roaring's heard from a sweetcorn lair.
Out, outdoor cucumber – back to the ridge
We've 'cues' so cool, they grow in the fridge.
Frankenstein food is here to stay
Men just had to mess with DNA
Those Doctors of Helix, bearded in stubble
What madmen, what sad men. Now we're in trouble!

Pests

Brown rot strikes the apple
Mildew shrouds the vine.
Pigeons gorge on cabbage plants
And rabbits wait in line.
Seymore revs his strimmer up
(He ain't no friend of mine).

Crane flies dress in leather jackets
As every gardener knows
Ratty winters in the compost
Black spot mars the rose.
Seymore whistles through his teeth
Everywhere he goes.

Wire worms in the Edwards
Green aphis curls the leaf
Blackfly is the gardener's curse
Cute nutkins is a thief.
Seymore's singing out of tune
Let's hope he keeps it brief.

Marestail is the worst of weeds
She brings much pain to us
Followed close by bindweed,
Nice name: Convolvulus.
Seymore's found that nettles sting
And don't he make a fuss!

The canker's in the parsnips
Bean weevil's in the beans
Carrot fly gets in again
By devious ways and means.
Seymore uses toxic spray,
Who could eat his greens?

Blackbirds ate the cherries
Listen to them chirrup.
Slugs n' snails stand against us
The badger beat us up.
Seymore sniggers, we turn green –
He's only won the cup!

Poetic Justice

Old Peg-Leg Pete, home from the sea
Tends his allotment plot.
No finer chap there'll ever be
And friends, he has a lot.

Fruit and vegetables fill his bowl,
He works with skill and pride.
Contented in his new found role,
In peace he does abide.

Then vandals struck one moonless night,
Laid waste to all he'd done.
With mindless nihilistic spite
In what they thought was fun.

The leader of this band of louts –
Six asbos bear his name.
With disregard what laws he flouts
Expects to take no blame.

But wait, he stole a rhubarb leaf
And chewed the toxic salad.
None but his Ma would cry with grief
To end a tragic ballad.

Thankfully the lad recovered,
Quite clearly saw the light.
Redemption at once discovered,
He toiled to put things right.

Snowdrops

Snowdrops formed in fairy ring,
Dancing fairies have their fling.
Bashful blooms nod white as snow
And radiate a pearly glow.
Harsh Winter's icy grip will bring
Promise of a kinder Spring.

A Reckoning

'Tis widely known that insects sting
And humans suffer burning pain.
Well, maybe there's a reckoning.

When bees and wasps are on the wing
There's every chance they'll sting again.
'Tis widely known that insects sting.

Winter yields to the warmth of spring.
Flowers display where snow has lain
Well, maybe there's a reckoning.

To old wives tales some old folk cling,
They trust in things beyond the brain.
'Tis widely known that insects sting.

But wait, is there not hope to bring
Where lasting goodness will remain?
Well, maybe there's a reckoning.

Sometimes natural cures are King –
Arthritis eased by venom's reign?
'Tis widely known that insects sting
Well, maybe there is a reckoning.

The Last Stone

It may well be my final pass
My aching joints despair,
Though how could I resist your mass
When I saw you lying there?
Heavy concrete paving stone
Impregnable, yet damaged too.
Imprudently risking broken bone,
I set to work on you:

With lever, guile and honest toil
I dragged you to my garden
Then stamped you down into the soil -
Might never earn your pardon.
Content you lie and face the sun
And I'm afraid my time has run.

The Bumble Bee

The bumble bee is a humble bee,
A rough and ready to rumble bee,
A never known to grumble bee.
The lazy sound of summer bee.
She's a freedom bee, flying free,
Won't live in hives or other dives,
Doesn't make honey for love nor money.
Can't be bought, sold, had, nor told.
No angry buzz, no barb'rous sting
Her captive cousin has to bring.
Down the years of evolution
She reigns Queen of resolution,
And pollination she has found
No problem on her daily round.

Lilac Spring

Quite suddenly as if prearranged
The lovely lilac catches our attention.
Winter's unkindly dreariness exchanged
For spring's freshly fragranted contention.
Once more abundant panicles pierce the green
As palest purple blossoms burst asunder.
The glad heart can pause by this winsome scene
And the soul upon its beauty ponder:
What power transfixes our perception
And brings fresh colour to our gloomy rooms?
This latest spring allows no exception,
Again it springs, and lo, the lilac blooms.
Tongue-tied lovers with speech so painful
Find gathering lilacs far more gainful.

A Sad Tale

A tree sugeon known as Stumpy Brandon
Plied his trade with gay abandon.
One careless stroke
On a stubborn oak
And he hadn't a leg to stand on.

Yew Trees

In the churchyard by the wall
An ancient yew tree green and tall,
A felon fell it,
But could not sell it,
Nor its berries steeped in gall.

In the graveyard by the gate
An ancient yew tree stands in state.
For thief or bard
Holds low regard
Where Nature's toxins regulate.

In the park's memorial keeping
Sculptured yew trees' silent weeping
Wash out the blood,
Erase the mud,
While the hound of war lies sleeping.

At another time in another war
Yew longbows drawn at Agincourt
Once felled our foes.
Ask god who knows
What use he meant dark yew trees for.

Apples Galore

Apples! Apples! Apples! Lying on the ground
In ever larger circles, begging to be found.

James might Grieve and Newton Wonder
At such prolific glut,
Abandoned, forsaken, strewn asunder
And trampled underfoot.

Bramley's Seedlings, Lane's Prince Albert,
Lord Lambourne's fodder for the fox.
Both culinary and lush dessert,
And you, you peerless Cox.

No molly coddling for Old English Coddling.
The Beauty of Bath falls on the path.
All this fruit, grown as a crop
Must it always be bought at a shop?

Why not take some to the food bank?
Hungry folk need must eat.
We have food, but we still thank
The Scrumptious windfall at our feet.

Moral:
An apple a day, keeps the doctor away,
Remember Doctor Crippen.
He forgot, it's sad to say,
To eat his Wyken Pippin.

"What Do Fish Know About Aquatics?"

It Happens – Naturally

A drop of water doesn't study hydraulics
As in a waterfall he frolics,
But joins his fellows in their revel
Cascading down to the lowest level.

Volcanic eruptions, thermodynamics
Raindrops on roses, quantum mechanics
Geometric perfection of high degree,
But how many snowflakes have a PhD?

The mighty oak of the genus *quercus*
Grows root and branch of generous radius.
They tap the moisture, absorb the light
Without a botanist in sight!

The majestic eagle soars on thermals
Never reads aeronautical journals.
His binocular vision developed in house
Spells the end of the fleetest mouse.

And what do fish know about aquatics,
Vulgar fractions or pure mathematics?
They know they're hungry and devour the fry.
It keeps 'em going, bye and bye.

But *homo sapiens* the naked ape
Sees the world a different shape,
By Curiosity he's held in thrall
Compelled to list and label all.

Before the final knell of doom
In some small white painted room
In deepest Hell's dark black bowl
Will, one day, dissect his soul.

The Mouse

Somehow, a mouse, got into the house,
Suffering cold and hunger.
At once we knew, what we had to do -
Visit the ironmonger.

The trap was set and we made a bet,
Would we be successful?
He took the cheese, took off on the breeze,
Leaving us distressful.

We, outdone, by a mouse on the run
More tightly tied the bait.
By the next morn, soon after dawn
We saw he'd met his fate.

Not being mice, it's really quite nice
To fear no retribution.
If hungry and cold, and getting old,
We face no 'final solution'.

Nutkins

Nutkins! What a handsome fellow you are!
Sitting so daintily chewing a nut.
Perfectly poised with tail in the air
Lost in the bounty of hazels in glut.
Now you are bobbing across the greensward
Dancing a ballet of balance and charm
To the place where your harvest is stored
Where you will endure and suffer no harm.
But the sun never shines with equal brightness.
Unhappy the lot your thin tailed brothers'
Blighted lives in perpetual darkness,
Dine on the dregs, the leavings of others.
Nutkins, be thankful and wave a fair tail,
Salute your good fortune. May it prevail.

Climate Change

Septober, Octember, no wonder
Gardeners through their beds a-blunder,
Head strong squirrels the hazels plunder
And wilful weather just falls asunder.

Reports come in of blossoming cherries
Mid November and sweet raspberries,
Daffodils and delphiniums all in bloom
Around our pond dragonflies zoom.

Shall we sharpen spades for the autumn dig?
Aye, and your knife for the ripened fig.
Marguerites still their flowers bequeath
Fresh poppies laid upon the wreath.

Tree pollen alergy's late this year
Something else for us to fear.
Now it's serious – it's just not right.
Aunty's got a mosquito bite!

Global Warning

What a wonderful world we live in
On that we all agree.
Full of Nature's treasures
Such rich diversity.

Of all the flora and fauna
Existing in this dream,
We are the world's most fortunate
And safely reign supreme.

Bestowed were we the finest brain
And hands to hold our tools.
Perhaps to reach beyond ourselves
To re-write Nature's rules?

We rapidly burn the fossil fuels;
Pollute the air and seas.
We are warming up the atmosphere
And cutting down the trees.

Man is riding his luck too far
The warning cries grow louder.
Ants will make this Earth their own
And sprinkle us with powder.

Weather Forecast

It will be dry in the morning with a
Few bright sunny intervals, cloudier later,
Then rain. Canute reigned but tamed no tide,
Thus Neptune's daughters entreat dear Pater
To place Siren Sisters on red alert
As the despondent low pressure slough,
Reminds folk scrambling on to higher ground
That barometers are redundant now.

While melting ice-caps swell the soulless Deep
Greedy men who present themselves as slaves
With empty posture lay a tawdry heap
Of sandbags alongside their certain graves.
Saint Swithin smiling on the raging spate,
Hears Neptune's daughters cry: too late, too late.

Red Roofs

Red roofs bear a leaden sky,
Heavy rain come Sunday.
Gale force winds expected by
Forties, Fisher, Lundy.

Red roofs reflect light on high
For springtime's verdant day.
Blossoms, bees and rosebuds vie
To welcome in the may.

Red roofs point to clear blue sky,
Summer's children play.
Earth's sturdy seedlings testify
Where lusty lovers lay.

Red roofs declare the house a home,
Hold close the warmth within.
The bee restocks her empty comb
And seals the honey in.

Sweet Dreams

The Queen is in her parlour
Eating bread and honey
Her Prince is in his chambers
Counting out his money.

The Chancellor's at the Treasury
Counting all our money.
The farmers in New Zealand
Keep sending us their honey.

The Chancellor takes a mighty cut
Of cash to fight the fiendish foe.
How come these endless enemies,
Does anybody know?

The Chancellor down in Downing Street
Chalks up a pound a litre,
You'll not be poor when I move next door,
No-one could be sweeter.

Soldiers wearing demob suits
Sit eating bread and honey
And the new PM has most sincerely
Pledged, to reimburse our money.

My Old Fence

The Sun comes out and dries wet wood,
Dry wood stands where wet wood stood.
The rain comes down and wets dry wood,
Wet wood stands where dry wood stood.

For most of the time I understood
That this was neither bad nor good,
But most of the time has since elapsed
And my old fence has just collapsed.

Wet Winter

Drenching, due to incessant rain
Farmers fume about unsown grain.
The Prime Minister speaks of 'biblical floods'
Fails again to deliver the goods.

No dredging done, no ditches dug
Planning? Down the drain, glug, glug, glug.
Make of this what you will,
And don't forget the water bill

Central Heating

The Romans had central heating
Many years ago,
When the communal bathhouse
Lay beneath the snow.

Two millennia forward
To a future fraught with folly,
Where those who sell the fuel
Enjoy monopoly.

To-day folk sit and shiver
By idle central heating.
They can't afford to have it on
And buy food for eating.

Morning's Child

It's time to rise, the sky is red,
The lark is singing way up high,
Life is too short to lie in bed.

You are hungry and will be fed
With tempting foods for you to try.
It's time to rise the sky is red.

Find ways dear child to bake your bread
And rise like it without a sigh.
Life is too short to lie in bed.

The alphabet from A to Z,
Will be as easy as apple pie.
It's time to rise the sky is red.

Your days beckon, they lie ahead,
The goods of life are there to buy.
Life is too short to lie in bed.

Seize the moment a wise man said,
There's much to do before you die.
It's time to rise the sky is red.
Life is too short to lie in bed.

Lost In Space

Scientists searching outer space
Deal with distance astronomical,
Seek spare room for the human race,
Something economical.

Presence of water is number one need,
A similar climate and size.
Too much to ask with mouths to feed?
Success requires no less a prize.

Could we ever quit this planet?
Have we brain enough to plan it?
Had we a ship, could we man it?
Can it be done? I ask you, can it?

Unlikely, as we spend more than earn
And wont to grasp beyond our reach,
Have such an awful lot to learn
And almost naught to teach.

Never finding what we seek
While through the void we plod,
May conclude our Earth unique
And never meet another god.

"And Feathers All A Fright"

Ragged Robin

A ragged robin ran round our feet,
Perchance to 'tice some morsel sweet.
For weeks on end our feathered friend,
Was there for us to greet.

His eyes were ringed around in white,
With some accursed avian blight.
Skull laid bare to the solar glare,
And feathers all a fright.

The once proud breast of robin red,
Was dull and drab. It must be said.
Preening feathers for all weathers,
Was no option. Most were shed!

Then off he slid this mortal coil,
His mouldering remnants in the soil.
Feeling sorrow, we knew for him no more tomorrow.
No more suffering. No fate disloyal.

Now we can say without correction,
There was a time of resurrection.
Come the spring when robins sing,
The flower of our affection.

Ragged robins do not die,
Their souls ascend beyond the sky,
Then magically one morn, return reborn,
To bloom where robins lie.

Lychnis Flos Cuculi:
Likes moist conditions only,
Prefers the shade of a damp green glade.
The shell pink flowers unruly.

The Sycamore Tree

Lodged high up in the sycamore tree
Big Black Crow looks down on the world below.
Robed in wisdom and authority, he
Studies humans scurrying to and fro,
Summons forth his Attorney General Rook
Whose knowing eyes contain all corvine lore,
Wearing fresh preened gown and learned look
Consults Lord Raven about looming war:
Full council's called and Magpies chatter,
Jackdaws veto collateral damage,
Top Jay bombers pinpoint windscreen spatter
Let the hawks of war stoop down in rampage!
While cruel Corvus cloaks his treachery
The stool pigeon hangs on the sycamore Tree.

Flight Path

As always was and shall be hence
That rush of wings and urgent cry
Migration follows the where and whence
The chevron skeins a lowering sky.
Arrowing low through twilight's glim
Sharing safe roost with kin at last
By urban lakeside's rushy rim
Find respite from the icy blast:
Primeval pilot take a bearing,
Come in Grey Leader, do you read me?
Your compass ancient and unerring
For ever set at ranging free.
Winging, calling from each Sun's rise
For ev'ry day until light dies.

The Magpie

Please don't persecute the magpie,
Leave him alone and let him be.
Ev'ry bird is protected by
RSPB.

Smartly attired like a waiter,
He welcomes all to the bird table
And dismisses cries of traitor
As old wives fable.

Bold and brassy, in no way weak,
Tho' does not peck beyond his dish,
Should not be hauled before the Beak
With prejudice.

The corvus family's comic crow,
Condemned by those who believe in elves,
Tells us all we need to know
About themselves.

Happy Bird Day

Long legged heron, never seen by Jack
Any coloured crow, so long as it's black.
Blue tits are blue (the name's the clue)
Hungry robins stay close to you.
The swifts are here but not for long,
While blackbird sings his tuneful song.
Hello woodpeckers down Woodpecker Way,
How much wood will you peck today?

Spot a shyly speckled thrush
Hiding under a gooseberry bush.
And here we have a collared dove
On wings of peace from heaven above.
Gentle Jesus starts with a 'J'
And you saw five the other day.
Rooks and pigeons up Betty's tree
Using the cars as a W.C.

Good morning, dear little Christopher Wren.
Hear the cackling from next door's hen,
Don't see much of our old friend starling,
Keep your pecker up, you old darling.
And sleek barn owl, you look nice,
We hope you take good care of mice.
So Happy Bird Day, enjoy a rest,
Tweet me from your cosy nest.

Not So Dumb

I see Leo and Larry
In friendly embrace.
Tigger licks Billy's
Sweet smiling face.

Fido brings Fi Fi
A huge bouquet
And Reynard takes Henny
Out for the day.

Crumbs of Comfort

We're now in good heart,
Five cats did depart,
All is peaceful and quiet.

The sparrows came back
And safe from attack
Enjoy their breadcrumb diet.

"In Our Hearts A Special Place"

Sarah 1

Sarah did her reading at Reading,
Towards higher things she was heading.
Then Gareth's computations,
Gave her further aspirations
And it's all ended up with a wedding!

Sarah 2

Shining eyes in a pretty face
Gleam as sunlight falls on water,
Windows to your inner grace,
Ready smile and joyful laughter.

You're running well Life's awkward race,
Never one to saunter,
In our hearts a special place
Our own, our darling daughter.

Karl

First born son lives down in Wiltshire
Having gained his own estate
Was at first too shy to venture
Much beyond the garden gate.

Each succeeding generation
Makes its mark with measured leap
Lifts its cap in veneration,
Hale memory of it's forebears keep.

While we, still till, the soil of Warwick
Your little sister lights a flame,
Your brother draws his columns doric
And much the world remains the same.

We love you Karl, our first born son
May fortune ever smile upon.

To Daniel

You always were a chatty child,
Argumentative, yes, but mild.
Now, true to plan,
A real first Dan,
Succeeds to hold us yet beguiled.

Kurt

Kurt felt the trigger on his Maxim gun
"Gott mit uns" on his belt lay writ.
Where is Tommy? I'll make him run!
But a three-o-three had *his* name on it.

Deep in his thigh with sharp pain sank
Bore him home beyond the fire.
Blessed belt, I have you to thank,
Yet my homeland dubs me "That Pariah".

'Thirty nine saw him seeking England's sanctuary
I'll join the army, more than willing,
Help build the camp quite voluntary
And wear your belt, it's worth the shilling.

Kurt felt the bullet buried deep
"Dieu et mon droit" his belt proclaims,
Truth lies still while millions weep
On gravestones burdened with countless names.

Written in fond memory of my father-in-law Kurt Ernst Lewin who fought in both world wars – on different sides. He had seven children, a bullet in his leg for 59 years and lived to the age of 95.

Christopher's Fifth Birthday

Well done Christopher – five on Friday,
You will be the 'Birthday Boy',
We all hope you have a great day.
You fill us all with pride and joy.

You love your Mummy and your Daddy
And brother Kieran too.
If only for your cherubic smile
We think the world of you.

Jill's 70th Birthday

You are doing well, you must be proud
The allotted threescore years and ten
Achieved, yet raise your voice to cry aloud
But this is now, and then was then!
The scribes of old who wrote the Bible
(God bless their quills and parchment)
Would this day be charged with libel
And ignorance of nourishment.
Here measured movement, balanced eating
Repeat the mantra five times a day.
Well wrought shelter, nothing fleeting
Holds rude nature firm at bay.
The outlook's clear, it must be said,
Your future stretches far ahead.

Father's Day

I remember in *my* father's day
When woodbine framed his door.
Then Time trotted through the mountains
To reach a distant shore.

I remember too the pillow
He plumped for his baby son,
For his curly headed baby boy,
Just as the world begun.

No more he sees his roses
No more sweet honeysuckle,
No more chuck the baby's chin
To hear his loin-fruit chuckle.

And now my sons remember me,
My garden fills with treasure.
Blossoms bloom and fragrant scents
Abound in equal measure.

I must entertain my grandsons
And chuck their chins some more
And smile away the hours
Before that not so distant shore.

"The Reaper Saw Our Brother"

In Memory of Alan

Red Rosehips were ripening fast
And beans stood tall and wide,
When the Reaper saw our brother
And bade him to his side.

Jenny Wren hid in the shed
The wind lay down and sighed,
And we were filled with emptiness
The day that Alan died.

Mischief twinkled in his eyes
Good fellowship his goal.
He always got us going –
The party's life and soul.

Stands he yet hard by the hedge
Whistling the Rudolf tune.
Should the morrow see his return
It would not be too soon.

Geordie Gordon

Geordie Gordon's not for glamour
Doughty son of Fishburn
Proven knight in shining armour
Turns wrongs to right in turn.

Shouldering half a dozen planks
Or spading tons of spoil
Here's a lad who asks no thanks
Marra, true and loyal.

Men like him are hard to find
England rues its lack
Tough outside, yet soft and kind
Upright, straight, broad back.

Salt of the earth we're bound to say
And down to earth as well
Bade farewell to the R.S.J.
And the coal black pits of hell.

Never slow to say his piece
He means just what he says
For him was writ especial lease
To him our special praise.

He stands foursquare to face the world
With cheeky Geordie grin
Presents his standard, proud, unfurl'd,
A man at peace within.

Gordon cleaved from a pea-pod cell
Dearly loves his brother,
Clearly unique, 'tis truth to tell,
There couldn't be another!

Joe

Big hearted Joe from big hearted Brum
Teaches Tai Chi with humour and skill.
Easing the tensions and toning the tum
He's top of the pops. Top of the bill.

He tells about the Chinese Legends
Of warlords loath to share their power.
We are his class, also his friends,
We gladly share his weekly hour.

Eyeballing practice – a fierce glare –
Is what we look at now.
Spending time in the Dragon's lair
Which ends up with a bow!

'Keep fit' too for the ancient limb
Joe steps up the pace.
Up, front, side, down – just like the gym,
Makes our pulses race.

The session ends with a bit of fun
Bean bags thrown with glee.
Joseph really is the one –
Worth twice his modest fee!

Harry's First Birthday

Congratulations, you have what it takes,
All hurdles cleared in the yearling stakes.
Let's drink a toast – your milk sup up,
You are just in time for the World Cup.

Your Mum and Dad are filled with pride,
Will you play one day for the England side?
With the Bard's lines a bond we forge,
Cry God for Harry! England and St. George!

It's In The Bond

Peter Barwell, "Bondy Pete"
No finer guy you'll ever meet.
When he's strapped into the pilot's seat
The throttle pedal sure feels the heat.

A chassis of steel and body of plastic
The underside is daubed with mastic.
Inside all's fixed with bits of elastic,
BUT, acceleration is quite fantastic!

Yet he's no roadhog, no Mr Toad,
He's the ultimate gentleman of the road.
Should you break down and need to be towed
He'll share your burden and lighten your load.

We see him stand in memory fond,
A man of his word and of his bond.

Birthday Ode to Betty

She floats on clouds of limpid light
Sweet wonders to behold
With firm belief in all that's right
As love and life unfold.
She plucked the flower of happiness
And tended well the bed
And walks in fields of friendliness
Where Angels lightly tread.

No-one we know can match your grace
Or be but half as good.
You show the world a smiling face
Your message understood.
Happy Birthday Betty, you're a treasure,
May this day bring you pleasure.

Aunt Jolly-Dee

My spiffing Auntie Jolly-Dee,
Is very fond of telling me
How often she has friends to tea
At half past three

She has some round at five as well
And seems to hold them in a spell
With talk of how they all look well,
So very well.

But Auntie has a darker side
Where she is anti-jolly dee.
Unfortunately, she can't hide
That side from me.

Fiona Denton

Feisty Fiona from Leamington Spa
'Could do better' and has, so far,
Only child of Dora and Teddy
Tho' daddy died before she was ready.
Nicely cultured, fountain of knowledge
Head girl elect at the Lady's College.

Red-eyed Dora to the station saw her
Off to Redbrick on the train
Proudly kissed her darling daughter
"Safely come you home again."

Fiona forbidden to play the street
Never a hop-scotch at her feet
Life's university opened her eyes
At every juncture a new surprise
Left leaning lad unzipped his plan
Clearly set out in the 'Rights-of-Man'.

Honours gained, lessons learned
An oystered world beneath her feet
A breast where all passions burned –
Enjoy, but 'ware, the waiting feast.

Che

A young revolutionary called Che
Had beaten the pigs in the bay.
Then while dancing the samba
He shouted CARAMBA!
And knocked all the drinks off a tray.

"From Civic Viewpoint On The Wall"

Not a Pronounced Success

A couple from Walsgrave-on-Sowe
Went for a row on Wyken Slough,
But the roe in their scoff
Was decidedly off
And the row ended up with a row!

War Memorial Memories

The Old soldier walks slowly
Through lines of cedar trees.
He hears a bugle calling,
Carried faintly on the breeze.

Now the sound of heavy guns
Rumble inside his head
And the screaming 'whizz-bangs'
Enough to wake the dead.

Deadly bullets from Maxims
Buzz like angry bees.
Our veteran feels a chill wind,
Cutting through the trees.

He remembers dreadful fear,
He remembers dreadful cold;
Every dreadfully long day
Until he's dreadfully old.

Old soldiers never die, it's said;
Their lives were theirs to give.
"Why would my comrades choose to die
When I was allowed to live?"

Dear Editor

You request we send our poems in
On any subject we may choose.
Did you cast my last into the bin
For expressing controversial views?
Enclosed within another verse,
To which I hope, you're not averse!

Camera Principis

Through grimy glass my glassy eye
Watches a worried world pass by.
I see the great, I see the small,
From civic viewpoint on the wall.

Zoom straight in on the teeming street
Trailing debris at its feet.
You laugh I see, black clad mourner
Stood with Crime at every corner.

I scan strong doors with triple locks
The outcast in his cardboard box,
Sub-zero nights in fetid socks,
His fearful friend, the urban fox.

See yon junkie splat his gum,
Misses me, and hits his chum.
Cocky in his back turned cap,
Clearly asking for a slap.

Now yobs riot in drunken rage
Writing tomorrow's dire front page.
Call 999, don't stand and gape,
Oh no! Dear me, I have no tape.

Underwent And Overcame

Ancient times saw our proud city stand
Amongst the noblest in the land.
    Godiva always guiding.

On whose bare shoulders justice sat
Shining standards to wonder at.
    Godiva fair, deciding.

Against oppression martyrs turned
Dragged screaming to the stake and burned.
    Godiva with sorrow siding.

Roundhead stronghold loved no King
'Sent to Coventry', no bad thing.
    Godiva e'er abiding.

Came the wars with little thanks
Motors, planes and armoured tanks.
    Godiva woe betiding.

Enemy action razed the city
Yet raised again – stay your pity.
    Godiva, were you hiding?

Now cheque book man whose shadow falls
Would want to breach these ancient walls.
    Godiva, are we riding?

Godiva – The True Story
(Now it can be told)

Our most gracious lady, Godiva,
Was a feudal financial provider,
She arranged rebates, in groats,
Her horse got some oats
And she lent her name to the 'Fiver'.

On that fateful day when she rode out
With ne'er a stitch, nor cloth nor clout,
Put wicked Leofric to shame.
But Peeping Tom took some blame,
Of that there is no doubt.

Tom, struck blind, was made to see
The error of his lechery.
And so today as we pass by
His mournful image raised on high
Celebrates his infamy.

The awful Earl ruled ruthlessly,
Treated the townsfolk disgracefully,
But his miserable life saw trouble 'n' strife
When outwitted by his own dear wife.
He should have been sent to Coventry.

Give the lad a chance

Paul's pa put him into painting,
Which filled him with revulsion.
What else was there for him to do?
His schooldays ended with expulsion.

They caught him simply *in flagrante*,
He had acted with impulsion –
Painting pink Frank Whittle's Arch:
The father of jet propulsion.

The Magistrates sat stony faced
And spluttered in convulsion.
"The Arch besmirched, he should be birched!"
Then retracted with repulsion.

"Clean up the mess and we'll not press
An order of compulsion,
As overcome you clearly are
With shocking pink emulsion."

Coventry 1983

Back in the summer of eight three
The sun shone down on Coventry.
On Coventry the sun shone down
And those that wanted got quite brown.

Baking cars in concrete lots
Sweating mothers, fretful tots.
Cursing fathers, craving beer
Wishing for another year,
To get them out this goddam spiral
Maybe Blackpool – perhaps the Wirral.

Redundant hopes, their futures pawned,
Brave new concrete city moulders.
Bitterness breeds where hate is spawned,
The dream breaks over rounded shoulders.

'Play up Sky Blues' – a pale lament,
'Pay up you slobs', a truer picture.
The krauts blitzed Cov. T'was their intent
But monetarists apply the tightest stricture.

Down Beat

Last night we went to Bedworth,
To hear the Black Dyke Band,
It were good to hear some northern brass,
And t'lads they played "reet grand".

It is a pity in Coventry city,
We could not hear their band,
At our very own civic centre,
Or at least, know one was planned.

But don't despair, we can stand and stare,
At the glorious Whittle Arch,
And perhaps a band of buskers,
Might strike up a Sousa march?

Nostalgia

Some talk of Alfred Herbert
And some of Francis Barnett
And some of Ena Sharples –
Resplendent in her hairnet.

Whistle Blower

Cardiologist, Doctor Raj Mattu,
Had a whistle which he blew,
On unsafe practice.
The Hospital Trust also knew
But sought to keep it out of view
And cause ongoing crisis.

Hospitals hold a duty of care
Which patients, staff and public share.
No remit to raise the wealth
Of suit, accountant or financier –
And drug companies embedded there
That poorly Service National Health.
Mammon needs extra tame apologists
More than useful cardiologists.

Windows To What

Three sad spires across the lonely city gazing.
Nightly viewers seek solace and inspiration
Tired eyes transfixed by double glazing
Their all consuming aspiration.
Art deco theatre razed, a tale of woe
The motor museum our proudest feature
Hey! Throw some craps in the new casino
While gibbering screens cloud our future.
Where now you Captains of yesteryear?
Quit those ghastly tombs, we need you back
Gone forever I suspect we fear
Lyons, Herbert, Wienstock, alas and alack.
"Export or Die" our Captains cried,
No more we toil yet something died.

Invalidity Street

Six little hospitals lived in the town
Then there were five. Well may you frown.
Because they aborted Maternity
For the rest of eternity.

Five little hospitals stood in a row
Then there were four - how do we know?
Because the Isolation site was cleared
And behold, a super-store appeared.

Four small hospitals left on the scene
Then there were three. See what I mean?
Couldn't *they* see by closing Paybody
A short-sighted move good for nobody?

Three small hospitals for our proud city
Then there were two, more is the pity.
Old and decrepit and has had it's day
The Gulson Road pile will just fade away.

Two infirmary places remain in the race
And one of those looks a terminal case.
Strangely, the one preferred by us all
Was the very same place the axe had to fall!

One of the best, superb, state-of-the arts,
Superhospital, complex sum of it's parts
Now stands alone in total splendour.
We are truly indebted to our PFI lender.

The Leofric Redemption

Godiva's well remembered fateful ride
Well filled our veins with civic pride.
Not so the Earl, her cheerless spouse
Brought scant cheer to the poor man's house.
Yet here this day, we can proclaim
The hostelry which bears his name
 Has found within its generous heart
Great joy to the city's poor impart.
A score plump fowls will grace the plate
Of those poor souls less fortunate.
Through the tireless toil of Cyrenian folk
Whose endless charity it doth invoke.
But one small doubt still troubles me.
Eight hundred, homeless, in Coventry?

The Severn Men

To observe them at work is sheer delight
Nothing deters them to go to such pains.
The men from the Trent are very polite.

Each man to his task quick-witted and bright
Well up for the job, their hands on the reins,
To observe them at work is sheer delight.

From cold morning's chill to sun at its height
All working, no cursing, no-one profanes –
The men from the Trent are very polite.

Their twenty ton truck is driven in right
From the highway down through narrowing lanes.
To observe them at work is sheer delight.

Up in our close and the parking's so tight.
Now they are poking and prodding our drains.
But the men from the Trent are *very* polite.

Power driven cameras find drains alright
And we're home and dry whenever it rains.
To observe them at work is sheer delight.
The men from the Trent are *very* polite.

The Waitress

Priscilla, Priscilla, the girl with the smile
Her feline features bewitch and beguile.
Hair jet black as raven's wings
Shows promise of a thousand things.

Warm brown eyes hold steady gaze,
Rapt attention never strays.
Strong white teeth define her most
Bid welcome to an ivory coast.

Our lissom lady presents the menu,
Pencil poised: "Between me 'n you
Sir, I'd buy myself a treat,
The fish's tastier than the meat."

Priscilla, Priscilla, we love her to bits,
When we dine at the Rep, it feels like the Ritz.
Oh beautiful Brummie, it's getting late,
You are the star - the table can wait.

Taken For A Ride

"PENSIONER'S BUS PASS GOES NATIONWIDE
JUST THE TICKET FOR THEM TO RIDE."
Headline news, quite sensational,
Lateral thinking. Most unusual!

Up to Headingley, watch the Test,
Or The Oval – whichever's best.
Study Oxford dons in cap and gown,
Enjoy 'Les Mis' in London Town.

Visit the family in Camberwell
With Uncle George and Aunty Nell.
Stand by Drake on Plymouth Ho,
Pack a case and off you go.

Down Pool Meadow booking seats
The sun comes up, the dream retreats
It's only 2008 you know
Free travel still has some way to go.

A way so full of twists and turns
Brings little joy and few returns.
Hang on to your zimmers, hold the euphoria
You must pay to reach Victoria.

Winding Down

In forty seven snow lay deep,
Harsh winter tarried long.
My father had a tryst to keep
    And I must tag along.

He had me placed a 'prentice lad,
At six halfcrowns a week.
My father was a kindly dad
    And I too shy to speak.

Work hard my boy and do your best
Rewards shall follow later,
And promise me you'll work with zest.
    Oh yes, I will, dear pater.

Thus duly down to Spon Street went
To languish with the clocks,
An industry in dire descent.
    I shuddered in my socks.

Poor pendulum, such tardy swing!
The hands of Time looked down
Yet yearned to see a warmer spring
    Throw off bleak winter's frown.

Unwound mainspring could you forgive
The wellspring's passing peak
When I was learning how to live
    On fifteen bob a week.

Purely Academic

At the grey treeless end of town
Wear your face of plastic
Don the cap and don the gown,
Play a role scholastic.

Eleven plus's no more in it
Grammar's looking tired
Comprehensive? Devil take it!
A 'cademy's been hired.

If I was at a 'cademy
I'd love ev'ry minute
And learn about a 'natomy.
It's all them bones. Init?

I'd scratch me 'ead an' do 'ard sums
Two plus two's my limit
But one can always count on chums,
That's the way *they* do it,

I would learn to talk real posh
Using words like 'ambit',
That one might make a pile of dosh
A profitable gambit.

The P.F.I has blazed a trail,
Fat cats stroke their fiddles
Pure piety finds holy grail
And expands their middles.

Cosmology's the life for me
Did 'Big Bang' begin it?
Comprehend theology?
That's the God's truth. Init?

Evolution? Revolution!
We want no part of that.
Men from space is our solution
Or God will eat his hat.

Creativeness is what we seek
(The Lord is on our side)
Inherited by you, The Meek,
Leaves others left outside.

Learn your tables, two times two
Repeat them 'till it's dark.
Read the fables about who made you
Prepare to board the Ark.

So there you have it girls and boys,
A 'cademy's will grace
Education's chalk-faced ploys,
Come, take your rightful place.

No more suffer long detention
No more the chas'ning rod
All we need's complete subjection
Before the seat of God.

A Bad Spell

Who put the 'Coven' in Coventry?
Where do witches meet at night?
Lucky Coventry has a rear 'entry'
Handy for hasty exit flight!

Where is the coven in Coventry,
Is it marked on the A to Z?
Do they break bread with the Gentry
Or feed where ghoulies fed?

First find the caldron, find the brooms,
Find the broomstick maker.
Catch them cackling in cold dank rooms.
Grill the undertaker.

Did they lay a curse on the Hippodrome
And blight the Smithfield Tavern?
Will ghosts forever Hales Street roam
In the shadow of The Raven?

Beneath the theatre's orchestral pit,
If legend tells it true,
Is where the witches spat their spit
And did what witches do.

"Needed Wheels To Get To Work"

Travelling On

My daddy's made a 'lectric car.
It's quiet and clean
And goes really far.
And you don't have a lot to pay,
Plug it in at night
And it's ready next day.

Daddy says we must cast off myopia,
We could be living in Utopia.
I love my dad, he's full of mirth,
He says the 'lectric car will save The Earth.

My daddy loves me, wants me to thrive,
Me and mine to stay alive.
He sees a world that's clean and good,
Without cars that run on oil and blood.

White Van Man

Smoky diesel, grimy paint,
Phone to ear and boot to floor,
Impatiently with bare restraint
Mocks the limits of the law.
In your mirror you will see him
Light a fag and flash his lights;
With narrowed gaze and jaw set grim
Aims to fix you in his sights.

Psychiatrists, in pure white coats
And social workers on his case
Confide together, comparing notes,
Seek to put him in his place.
Where humble folk and not so bold
Might choose to hear *his* story told.

Road To Nowhere

Sleek, powerful, purposeful machine
Crouched, ready to race down The Drive.
A change of gear in wealth there's been,
Move over there, please stand aside.

Multi cylindered, countless valves
Four by four via six speed box
All egos firing, no conscience salves.
Ambition into the fast lane locks.

Sumptuous chrome leather seating
Nineteen inch alloys hug the bends
Testronic levels checked and meeting
Fully loaded means and ends.

Accelerating through the froth of nowhere
Grip the wheel with sweaty hands
Tell me, now, it's leading somewhere
With chequered flags and cheering stands.

The People's Car

At first, of course, I wanted
A Jag or Merc
But needed wheels
To get to work.
Then I saw you in a sale,
Affordable car, you were, you are
An affordable car.

You held promise of exciting journey,
Cortina, Granada, along the
High Sierras to Capri
And the multi-storey car parks
In the near vicinity.

Yes, I remember the Dagenham Dustbin
Rocking, rolling, rattlin', rustin'.
Now all lads and ladettes have one,
Where's the freedom, where's the fun?

They Don't Make Cars Like That Anymore

We set out for London in the Silver Eagle,
Dauntless like Darwin on the Beagle.
Before the M1 had yet been built,
Down the old Watling Street at full tilt.

The Alvis men at the local factory
Thought the cooling system satisfactory,
But when St. Albans hove in sight
The engine was smelling hot and tight.

Eagle's radiator, boiling, steaming
What a nightmare! Was I dreaming?
What engineer, what sort of man
Would design a motor without a fan?

Going Nowhere

Jaguar, Peugeot down the road, after Rover
Into casino fields of clover
Cards and dice
Shades of vice
A man once turned those tables over.

A Prize Pothole

Poor rutted road, its tarmac split,
A prize pothole, a yawning pit.
It fills with cars,
And old jam jars.
The council's looking into it.

"Then John Met Yoko"

East Meets West

In Samurai frown
Poet Basho's leaving town
To a silent sound.

Where, why, which and when?
Fate's finger may point and then
Split the minds of men.

Are you red, or blue
Grandest Master of Haiku
How do we know you?

With naked haiku
Can you tell us something new
Or our bards undo?

We unchain the pen
Relax the line, brook no yen
For too brief zazen.

Then John met Yoko
Made music (without Ringo)
Never said O no.

Lady and Lennon
Like the mortice and tenon
Born to be as one.

Fond Dreams

Now I know that fond dreams disappear with the dew
As the cold morning light shows clear.
But the bee to the blossom has vows to renew
When she whispers consent in his ear.

Will you have me and hold me in the heat of the day
Then straight away set to depart?
Though she knew the right answer and the price that you pay
For happiness sown in your heart.

Now we know that fond dreams only rarely come true
And we really shouldn't think that they will,
But hope springs eternal, our reward's overdue
And our appetite yearns for it's fill.

The sun's at it's height in the heaven above
It will sink in the westering main.
If the hardness of daylight engenders no love
Soft moonlight prompts dreaming again.

The Food Of Love

You're a vegetarian
And live on beans and bran.
I'm a Sagittarian,
A meat pie munching man.
You like new potatoes
And vegetable marrow.
I know where the rabbit goes,
He will know my arrow.

For sure there is a heaven
Much nearer than the stars,
When after tea at seven
We share your minty bars,
Then beneath a cheesy moon
Get to grips with the pickle spoon.

First Steps

Put on your flip-flops
Put on your shoes
Let's go down the pop shop
And get some booze.

Alco-pop's cool
Alco-pop's nice
Cool boys rule
Girls entice.

Some has the vodka
Some has the rum
Exotic elixir
(Don't tell Mum).

Alco-pop's sweet
Alco-pop's good.
Strut that street
Snog that hood.

High upon your heels
Higher than you think
That's the way it feels –
You need another drink.

It Takes Two

Nothing's as dead as the dodo,
Where did it leave its libido?
When did all passion go out of fashion,
How could it wish to fly solo?

Nothing's as dead as the dodo,
Why put love on embargo?
What's wrong with wooing or billing and cooing,
Who was the first to say no no?

Nothing's as dead as the dodo,
Lifeless and lower than limbo.
Off dropped their wings and other dead things
Would never thrill to a tango.

Nothing's as dead as the dodo,
Oh for a fiery fandango!
Didn't they care for the habits of cute little rabbits,
Why weren't the males more macho?

The music died with the dodo,
A wake instead of a mambo.
Backs turned on romancing. Strictly no dancing,
Sadly, they all had to go go.

Sweet Heart

Love is like a cup of tea
Me for you and you for me
No added sugar required you see
Our love's as sweet as it can be.
As the golden grape clings to the vine
Begs description to define
Outside the scope of poetic rhyme
Sweetness beyond the word divine.
Is it possible to more refine
And turn that sweetness into wine?
We would not want nor so incline
My love is yours and yours is mine.
Years ago we saw a sign
Which bid us both our hearts entwine.

"Forfar Five, East Fife Three"

Come On England

Come on England, come on Sven,
Fear not Klinsmann nor his kinsmen.
Carve your names in marble halls,
Think of leather boots and balls.
Invoke the spirit of sixty six,
Draw inspiration from the phoenix.
It was done before by Alf Ramsey's men.
Hardly the League of Gentlemen.
That toothy grin from hardman Nobby,
Mrs. Charlton's Jack and Bobby.
And Bobby Moore – he was great
Made Eusebio look second rate.
Hero Hurst our hat-trick ace
Put the Germans in their place.

Come on England, come on Sven,
Play with pride. You are Englishmen!
They fired the turnip and hired the Swede,
Think of glory, not of greed.
Your exploits fill the tabloid pages,
But now it's time to earn your wages.
Ramsey's men played with pride and passion,
Now it's more to do with fashion.
Media tales of unseemly lives,
Lurid details of footballers' wives.
Become the men your dads begot,
Not the boys that time forgot.
Let not memories of Gazza's tears
Mean another forty, hope dashed years.

American Soccer

We played the game and we walked tall
From boy to man we knew our role
Now Uncle Sam wants our football.

Smart talkin' dudes with a yankee drawl
Snake oil salesmen aint got no soul
We played the game and we walked tall.

Star spangled stadia midst urban sprawl
Hallelujah and welcome to the Superbowl
Now Uncle Sam wants our football.

Green astro turf from wall to wall
And wider posts for the easy goal
We played the game and we walked tall.

"Your old world ways could use an overhaul
See the leggy cheerleaders toss that pole."
Now Uncle Sam wants our football.

"Tell us what you think of our cute new ball,
Your Executive Board sits, on a grassy knoll."
We played the game and we walked tall
Now Uncle Sam wants our football

A Football Match

What we want is a football match.
When the drums beat and the bugles call,
Too urgently our foes dispatch.

In no-mans land some respite snatch,
Find yourselves a neutral football,
What we want is a football match.

Our goal should be to start from scratch
And rid the Jingo of his gall.
Too urgently our foes dispatch.

A half closed door held on its latch;
Penalties paid while loud mouths bawl,
What we want is a football match.

Hedge fund killings designed to catch
The long and the short and the tall.
Too urgently our foes dispatch.

Now long in tooth and short of thatch,
Held tight in summer's humid thrall.
What we want is a football match.
Too urgently our foes dispatch.

Scottish Score Line

Forfar five, East Fife three
For Brechin bairns the milk comes free.
As Rabbie loved his red, red rose
They love free prescriptions in Montrose.
And they're nae so dumb in old Dumbarton
More free milk, by the carton.

Rangers and Celtic the 'Old Firm' marvels
Carved in stone like Elgin's marbles.
Hamilton Academicals, students of chemicals
Are more at ease without tuition fees.
North of the border in Stenhousemuir
Prime Angus sizzles on the skewer.

Sassenachs spout stuff about Gordon's fault,
Canny Jock smiles and sips his malt.
Hear the skirling pipes alilt,
It's Scots wha' hae – and up your kilt!
East Fife four, Forfar three,
England penalised – Scots, scot-free.

Skin Deep Boots

He's only wearing skin deep boots,
Heroic forward checks, spins and shoots.
In Football's pretty packaged parcel
You'll find a fractured metatarsal.

Sponsors pay him loads of money,
Tragic, if it weren't so funny.
Why, when affording Armani suits
He's only wearing skin deep boots?

"....The Clocks Straight Off The Wall"

A New Day

A first faint light the heavens brush
Foretells departing night once more,
Before the earliest glint of morning's blush
Bedecks my bedroom floor.

Soon sweet Dawn her curtain draws
Away dark shadows of the night.
She plaits ribbons of expectant pause
And prepares the world for light.

Blackbird brooding on the fence sits still,
Awaiting inspriration he assures us,
Then treats us to symphonic thrill
With the new day's opening chorus.

Through my window the first rays steal,
Warmth and light enjoined as one.
New joy, fresh hope our thoughts reveal
A new day has begun.

Father Time

In the spring and in the fall
We take the clocks straight off the wall.
Put them forward. Turn them back!
No power the Powers would seem to lack.

Our summer's bloomed and sadly gone,
Winter's shroud ready sewn to lay upon
Shoulders bent through this vale of tears.
Would the Powers, turn back the years.

"Black Witches Of Doom"

Halloween

Halloween again. Cauldron bubbling,
broomstick propped by the door, as usual.
Only this Halloween was going to be very
special....

Camera, lights, action!
Actors aping putrefaction.
'Cryptwriters have us all in stitches,
Banshees, ghoulies, ghosts and witches.
Electricians, 'grips' in woolly hats
Get to grips with cool black cats.
Make-up girls applying gore,
Director checks rhubarb wine and gingerbread store.
Halloween party's going great –
£3.50 at the allotment gate.

Halloween 2007

The kids loved going trick or treating at Halloween
but no-one ever dared call at the house on the hill…

Only fools and strangers
Enter the house on the hill
And know the malign presence
Of pure evil.
A tramp blundered in
More numbskull than most
Flew out demented
When he saw the ghost.
Sweet innocent girl child
Legend says died
Where she stood stricken
And petrified.

Diabolical Trick

Halloween Night, black witches of doom
Stealthily glide to far off lands.
Seeds of destruction spawned of the tomb,
Pregnant pumpkins flown to innocent hands.

Babies (bright orange), born with the day,
Children drawn to bundles of joy.
Babies erupt in fireworks display,
Children dismembered, no lives to enjoy.

"The Wheel Wins"

You Bet

Casinos Inc. seek high permission
To guarantee best profits yet
In such a juicy proposition
Will they invest? You bet!

Turn the card, throw the dice
Play James Bond, suave and cool
Take a lady, treat her nice
Pretend you're no deluded fool.

Round and round the wheel spins
Stop for me, our punter prays
The wheel stops, the wheel wins
Pound and punter go separate ways.

Lady Luck her bounty strews
Along the driveways of the rich
Luckless dreamer doomed to lose
Trudges home with bare a stitch.

Instant wealth is but illusion
Learn that well and don't forget
See it clear without confusion
Where they invest – you bet.

The Loser

It's not immoral, immoral it's not
I lay my bets and nobody cares.
My stakes are small, but they're all I've got,
It's not immoral, immoral it's not.
I should know better, but I don't, so what?
Who knows which face the Devil wears?
It's not immoral. It's not, it's not!
I lay my bets and nobody cares.

"....Flying Dentist Fell Out With Gravity"

What A Pantomime

Alas and alack, the Belgrade's not ready,
The galloping millions are making us heady.
The panto cancelled – we feel undone.
But the real pantomime has aleady begun.

Richard Whittington turns to his cat:
"I wonder what they're playing at?
Many a long year we trod the boards,
Folk flocked to see us in their hordes."

The wise cat turns to Dick:
"Yes, it really does make one sick,
The Hippodrome demolished, brick by brick,
Replaced by a clock that doesn't tick!"

In a councillor's eye not yet a gleam,
No stirring of a contractor's team?
To plan and build a new civic hall,
Will we never, ever have one at all?

So turn again Whitty, head back down South
We're not completely down-in-the-mouth,
We know such a lovely resourceful pair
Will send us fun from Albert Square.

Animal Crackers

It takes two to tango
Said the ostrich to the snail
And the aardvark close behind me
Is reading all my mail.

That's nothing said the badger
And shook his two-tone head.
They say TB or not TB
But I think they want me dead.

Down among the dandy lions
There dwells a four eyed rabbit.
I always say, four carrots a day
Is foresight's healthy habit.

What's it all about then?
Thought the dogfish in the Sherbourne,
I'll poodle down to the nail-bar
And have my fins sprayed auburn.

No night mare dreamt so strange a dream,
Where she led round Tattenham Corner,
Ridden by a guy with a Christmas pie
And he was little Jack Horner.

Emergency Poetry Service

When your mantel's overflowing
With ever mounting bills
And Trouble's pressing down on you
With it's ever urgent ills.

When your fences keep on falling down
And the old man's down the pub,
Young Wayne is on an ASBO
And Tracy's in the club.

When the box is on the blink again
And dishes pile the sink
And Fido's done a 'whoopsie',
Then it's time to stop and think.

You have had it up to here with life,
So call the Emergency Poet.
He will take your mind off things –
You'll be smiling before you know it!

Press one for a funny limerick.
For odes of love, press two.
Press three and four for much, much more.
There's something just for you!

Filling His Last Cavity

The Flying Dentist fell out with gravity,
His name was Phillip George McCavity.
It's the sad but honest truth,
He won't pull another tooth
And no more Phil McCavity.

Shelley Vision – A Parody

Wall to wall programs just about cookin'
So decent material can't get a look in,
Over tarted food lies like lead in the belly.
Clear the canteens for the vision of Shelley.

There are cops and robbers in unvanquishable number
Going round in tight circles like drunks after slumber.
Heavy weight pundits dissemble the news
With depressingly familiar BBC views.

Adverts and trailers we would rather not view.
Complaints are too many, improvements too few.
Pointless celebrities, famous for being famous
Say, "We're making money! How can you blame us?"

Time for our hero, please meet Percy Bysshe;
A man of integrity and girls find him dishy,
Not part of a dinosaur dynasty,
But someone to trust with the licence fee.

We'll have education for breakfast and laughter for tea,
Ethics for supper and organics come free.
Philosophy, literature and men with a mission.
Be sure to look into the new Shelley Vision.

The Importance of Sharing

When first I met my true love
My heart she promptly stole.
My proposal met her approval
And marriage was our goal.
Always had I been somewhat thrifty,
We would share things fifty fifty.
So when we share a polo out
I get all the mint
And she gets all the hole!

Ode To The Cliché

They have crucified the cliché
They've cut her to the quick.
Her street talk lip is so passé,
Don't they take the mick!

All shoulders to the wheel my lads,
A damsel's in distress.
No Hall of Fame for her – the cads!
She's wearing last year's dress.

So, put it on the back burner?
No, stare it in the face.
She's a trouper, cool head-turner,
She always holds the ace.

Old saws and sayings are lauded
All comes out in the wash.
The cliché's never applauded –
Always under the cosh.

See the elephant in the room,
Take her to your bosom.
Try sweeping cleanly with new broom
Go and kiss your cousin.

Oh take me in your arms again,
The science isn't rocket.
Stay close to me, I share your pain
And the pound in your pocket.

We ought to give thanks to the cliché
In helping our over strained wit.
When we struggle with something to say
She already has words for it.

Tough Call

Girls who touch up their lippy in public
And do it while driving are mad.
And guys who use mobiles
When driving automobiles
Are also, quite equally bad.

But as citizens solid our duty is clear,
We must report these two bounders –
Such blighters surround us,
And we could be 'Snitch of the Year'
I fear,
And you would be snitch of the year.

Memory

They tell me I've left my lights on again
The coffee break I must forsake.
My short term memory becomes a pain
More care in future must I take.

Last night I stood at the privy door
No lock could find, not yet a key.
The more I thought, my memory's poor,
There is no lock on the lavatory.

Hats Off in Court

No berets, no bearskins
No birettas or wimples
Young ladies look better
When showing their dimples.

Let's ditch the deerstalker
The chav baseball cap –
And the Arch Bishop's mitre
Must sit in his lap.

We ought ban the sombrero
The fez and the turban,
The fedora, the trilby,
So awfully suburban.

And we won't allow helmets
(Motor-cycle or pith).
If I had a say
We would give them a miss.

None of your faces
Shall lurk 'neath a mask.
How much less of a favour
Could we possibly ask?

So off with the hoodies
Off with the veil.
And leave your fine wig sir,
Up high on it's nail.

Living Language

When I was but a tousled lad
My dad would fondly say,
It's up to you my son
Just how you make your way.

Much water 'neath the bridge has flowed
And words have flown to toe from head.
Now it's down to you my dear old friend
To judge the life you've led.

When maid and swain in days gone bye
Were in a hay loft found,
'Twas said they'd had it off, you know,
A phrase that's losing ground.

In these enlightened modern times,
Are those with broad agendas,
Whereof we hear they get it on.
Oh please, dear Lord - defend us!

Modern Times

Pedestrian poetry, clipperty clop,
The tortured line and abrubt full stop.
Shakespeare spinneth in said grave,
From Johnny-come-lately literati save.

Songbirds singing, sweethearts clinging,
Kylie's partying through the night.
Mobiles ringing, birthdays bringing
Reasons to purchase all things bright.

Instant credit, direct debit,
Celebrities show the dot-com paths.
Faxes, texts – whatever next?
Rich men stifle belly laughs.

Cruel talon in latex glove,
Clawing down the culture.
On hold, sweet dove with heaven's love,
Behold! The Devil's vulture.

The Poetry Class

Tutor calls for a super sonnet
John peers out through jaundiced eye
Lucy has lost her poets bonnet
Rob's quill lies still, clean and dry.
Linda prepares for examinations
Tim books a session with his muse
Mary spends time on long narrations
Richard's limericks must amuse.
Can Jackie rescue us from despair?
Has Nadine hidden latent genius?
Will Peter suddenly punch the air
With inspired lines to save us?
Poetic licence outruns its lease
The immortal Bard can rest, in peace.

Persuasion

Can I persuade thee now to shun pork chop?
No more thy finger licking joy explore,
Not one more chicken nugget slyly pop
Into that spacious all consuming maw?
Remember roasting beef with BSE?
Which swelled the gut and plumped the tum
And fatted the calf of thee and me,
O'er filling our veins with unctuous gum?
Self-indulgent, drawing shed-load salaries
Blissfully denying arterial hard'ning,
Shouldn't you be counting mounting calories
And giving thought to vegetable gard'ning?
Fat's not funny, it lies beneath the joke,
Withholds lifeblood and future, at a stroke.

Blake's Heaven

And did those feet in metric time
Walk upon England's mountains green?
And was the Holy Lamb of Blake's rhyme
Laid with mint on platters seen?

And if the Countenance Divine
Shone no light on our clouded hills
Then who would want Jerusalem builded there
Among those dark satanic mills?

Bring me my bowl of red hot curry!
Bring me pints of Sainsbury's mild
Guide my arrows, sweet Ruby Murray!
Dear Mother England! I am your child.

I will not cease from mental fight
Nor use my sword on Darwin's monkey.
O.K. build Jerusalem, it's quite alright,
But *please* don't bring the donkey.

Blood Tests At Tesco

Get all your blood tests at Tesco
Along with the lamb and the pork,
When you've stocked up on wine and tobacco
Then go for your clinical talk.
You sail down the aisle with detergent
Select your fresh veg from a pile,
But if your medical need is urgent
You can head for the nurse with a smile.
Loo rolls and toothpaste are chosen
Very little stays long on the shelf,
You are happily to Tesco beholden
In return, they look after your health.
They'll test your blood for a nominal fee
There's no need to book and the parking's free.

Plastic Wrapping

Plastic bags mus'tek da rap
For da fishy mek a trap,
Cloggin' deltas an' bus sheltas
Roun' da street al' helta-skeltas.

In lan' fills an' fishy gills.
Dus' bin spills an' birdy kills
Blockin' rivers blockin' drains
Causin' floodin' when it rains.

In da groun' dey ain' degradin'
Yo ken 'ardly get yo spade in,
Med from oil, spoil da soil
'Al da toil mek mi boil.

We doan wan' no plastic bags
Killin' cormorants n' shags.
Dey say dem las'a t'ousan' years
Mus' do, got to, end in tears.

Kitchen draw's filled to bustin'
An' da shed, an' da dus' bin.
Ten k bags in de attic
'Comes a monster, got attack it.

Hey man! Get yo brain cell movin'
We mus' do a bit improvin',
Reusin' paper is da Road
Startin' wi' dis tatty ode.

Beautiful World

Poets pretty ditties pen
Never asking who, or why,
or what, or when.
No boats rocking,
No horns locking,
No politics mocking,
or snoots a-cocking.

Nature's natural,
Who would deny it?
Love is lovely,
We all try it.
But right is right
And wrong is wrong,
The crow sings a dreadful song.

Pure White Teeth

Poutable lips, open wide mouth
Sixteen above, sixteen beneath
Half in the north, half in the south
Rows of white teeth.

Incisive incisors, angled chin.
Row upon row, parade ground style,
Lethal canines contained within
Her feline smile.

Molars meant for mastication,
Mouth watering sweet meats to chew.
Could you spin words in fabrication?
I can. I do!

Each new exposure to your pearls,
Renders men mere bowls of jelly,
But putty in the grip of girls
On the telly.

One must project oneself when young.
Go, sing your song of self belief,
Climb the ladder, hang on each rung
With pure white teeth.

Solutions

Slid through my letterbox one day
A brochure on the doormat lay.
Full of solutions to cure all ills
Like cleaning plastic window sills.

Wonderful, wonderful, wonderful world
Of gadgets and gizmos now unfurled.
Linoleum floor polish and non-slip mats,
Strong smelling vapours will scare off cats.

Handy shoe rack with chromium rails.
Long handled clippers for tough toenails,
Super plasters soothe sensitive toes,
Bug killer zaps flies and mosquitoes.
Freestanding wardrobe for my smart clothes,
I-pod for music "wherever she goes."

Ergonomically designed shopping cart
Electronic ear cleaner. Twenty one pin scart.
Cordless, electric cylinder mower,
No need for a man, he was a goer.

Vinyl soft packs of waterproof pants
A powder dispenser to deal with the ants.
Flattering fuller figure controlling bra,
Lifting the spirits and raising the bar.

A perfect oven for a perfect tart,
Why, oh why, did he have to depart?
Why don't you stock a painful dart –
Or something to fix, a broken heart?

Psycho Babble

The Ego, Superego and Id,
Trip a Viennese Waltz.
So please don't forget to tell Sid.
They'll cure his mental faults.

Manny Kant's stripped down to his pants
Old Jung is in his prime.
Sex reigns supreme, Doctor Freud rants,
It really is sublime.

When the Jungmann's washing his kecks
Pavlov's training his mutts.
Ziggy Freud treats oedipal wrecks
While Kanty strains his guts.

Dreams and childhood cause contention.
Like reading blots of ink.
Let's hope that anal retention
Will not cause too much stink.

The Agony Auntie's of tabloids
May claim to lift male droops.
Though more likely set off haem'rhoids,
With looks like Margy Proops.

A psycho-somatic minefield –
Just relax on the couch.
The wormholes in mindsets revealed –
Control your Ego slouch.

Sigmund Freud, C. Jung and E. Kant
Sadly, forgot to tell Sid.
Did shekels underlie their want?
Who did they hope to kid?

Zog

There was an old caveman called Zog
Who went on a date in the fog
They met by a boulder
She'd only one shoulder
And a face like the back of a dog.

Christmas Thoughts

Let peals ring out at Christmas time,
Let tills and sleigh bells jingle.
May friends and families be as one
And children feel the tingle.

Hark ye back to Christmas past,
They will not come again,
Cabbage Patch Dolls, Ninja Turtles
And the dear old 'Mr.' Men.

The brewery's working overtime –
A million gallons more!
Muscats flown in from the Argentine,
Delivered to your door.

Gobble down the turkey.
Greasy fingers lick,
Then watch the magic mince pies
Do their disappearing trick.

And should He return on this his day,
Would He be filled with gladness,
Or shake his head in disbelief
And plumb the deepest sadness?

Once before He showed the way
True happiness to find,
To share things out to each and all,
To the whole of humankind.

The Feast of Stephen

Praying mantis arn't known for grievin'
And she was hungry for her Steven.
She bit him, he died,
She fancied him fried –
Deep, and crisp, and even.

Reliable Sources

A reliable source is the horse's mouth,
He can outpace a rocket.
Yet punters seldom beat the odds
And end up out of pocket.

The politician's a reliable source.
A font of inside knowledge,
Finally spells out the wicked cost
To see the kids through college.

Your employers, another reliable source
Keep in touch without fail.
When your position becomes redundant
They send you an email.

Parents, you'd think, a reliable source,
Larkin said they fuck you up.
Basically then, you won't succeed
And never win a cup.

The most reliable sauces known to man;
Spicy brown, from the Brum factory
And delicious red tomato ketchup
Both, entirely, satisfactory.

"Greed Is Good"

Greed Is Good

Greed is good the lady said,
It makes a mighty nation.
All power to the notion,
Of solid wealth creation.

She scorned the voice of elders,
Not to flog the family plate.
She would wear the trousers
And then went on to state:

There is no society,
We have another creed,
We till the soil of enterprise,
We sow a different seed.

With Christian ethics written off
Society ceased to be.
Human values laundered out
Into a swamp of money.

Money so devalued,
Printed by the ton,
Representing piles of debt,
No use to anyone.

Should Do Well

He must take the Hypocritic Oath
And sign the Pact of Lies
Enter the chamber of that ancient place
Where Truth lays down and dies.

He needs per-fect the art of lying
In particular through his teeth
That fools about from north and south
See not, what lies beneath.

He shall speak of democracy and freedom,
Free speech, equality and social justice.
Heed not dear friend, lest we should end
With ever more injustice.

He may wear a flaming red rosette
Or one of truest blue,
Or one so made with any shade
Which might appeal to you.

He will stoop to kiss the babies
And shake the crushing hand,
Prepare to share a bed or gutter
With the lowest in the land.

Notice how his lips are smiling
Though his eyes in stone are set,
While he cuts sweet deals with the Devil
And the foulest deeds beget.

When all is cooked and honeyed
He could gain his life's ambition
And reach his goal in the starring role
Of perfect politician.

Justice Delayed

First let the trail go stone cold
Pack the bloodhounds off to bed
Put all urgent calls on hold
Deal the cards, black and red.

Let the evidence go astray
Feed the newshounds what they crave
Watch witnesses walk away,
Titbits for tomorrow save.

Footprints fade with turn of season
Though the foxhounds scent their prey,
Notebooks stored, without good reason?
No, they will see the light of day

When placemen checking dusty diaries
Fearing wolfhounds at the gate
Announce at last delayed enquiries
And leave the scapegoat to his fate.

Progress 2005

Ancient man devised a plan:
He needed to be inventive.
Survival was the sharpest spur,
A down-to-earth incentive.

First a circle in the sand,
Then he made a wheel.
And soon he's circling round the globe,
In mighty ships of steel.

Wondrous cities sprang up from deserts,
Arts and science flourished.
Plough and trawler were the means.
To see all peoples nourished.

There we were in paradise,
In lands of milk and honey.
But oh the cracks began to show,
When we invented money.

Much of the world's in poverty,
And misery and debt,
Homeless, starving, war-torn,
That's what the losers get.

While we fret about our waistlines,
Yet pile into the pubs,
Then burn the surplus calories off
In trendy fitness clubs.

"Shop until you drop" we're told,
With credit cards a-quiver.
Live today, forget tomorrow,
The Market will deliver!

Modern man has no plan,
There is no point he feels.
And spends his days just circling round,
On polished alloy wheels.

Taxing Times

Friends, Brits, Countrymen,
Lend me your ears.
Is our tax system not progressive?
Please allay my fears.

VAT is paid by all
From lord to lowly peasant,
From those who most likely have
And those who certainly haven't.

Compare your non-dom billionaire,
(whose tax comes duty free)
With the lucky man in a job
Caught in PAYE.

Why not level the playing field
And play a fairer game?
If we are all in it together
Why do the poorest take the blame?

Chancellor, square that circle
Into a democratic fit,
Then by George, by jingo,
There would be no deficit.

House Of Cards

Bluecoat blazered, button down collars
Hear them shout across the floor
Electronically liquefying petro-dollars
Hyping junk bonds evermore.
Daily slog on the City's bourse
Ever climbing vertiginous debt
Never to be repaid, of course
Leveraged buy-outs, more hedge funds yet.

Leering down from his advantage
On his lackeys in the pit
Mamon's fortunes take no hostage –
Oh, the rapacious fun of it!
As towers fall in crumbling shards
Who will trump the losing cards?

Safe As Houses

Along primly ordered avenues
Around the corner by the park,
Neatly trimmed herbaceous borders
Row on row down Primrose Walk.

Pebble dashing thirties semis,
Morris Oxford on the drive.
Little wifey in the kitchen,
Hubby working nine till five.

Good foundations, English bonded
Well cemented London stock.
Heavy ridge tiles firm, withstanding
Cold northern winds attempt to rock.

Bank of England's Grand Old Lady
Holds council in Threadneedle Street.
Sheltered behind those fulsome skirts
Our faith in her is quite complete.

Unfit For Purpose

Hard Times are not so hard to see.
Credit. That glib seducer!
Borrowed coinage: brass, bread, lolly,
Sometime filthy lucre.

The sweated wedge to banks we tote,
They smile through whitened teeth,
In tiny print the mortgage wrote
And bonded fast beneath.

Their light touch, light foot, hedging fleet,
Those slick self-serving elves
Deemed fit by friends in Downing Street
To regulate themselves.

Save the World

Please save the world Mr President, Sir,
You have the time and skill. We are aware
As Commander-in-Chief the power too.
Stand by the American People who
Ache deep within their fervent hearts to see
Goodness shine through dark clouds of enmity.

Freedom, Democracy, twin restless wraiths
Entwine with Liberty a myriad faiths.
Since Gettysburg witnessed Independence born
To your finest hour on the White House lawn.
Throw shoes at failure, aim for higher things,
Listen to created equal fellow beings.
Lincoln, Jefferson, FDR stood tall,
Obama can, no SHALL, surpass them all.

Dear Uncle

Uncle Sam, Uncle Sam,
We cling to you dearly
And we've found that your
         jeans fit us well.
But could burgers and coke
         be your little joke
Now our tummies have started to swell?

Dearest Uncle, dear Sam,
We dance to your music.
You introduced us to rhythm and blues.
You gave us your soul
         and your rock and your roll
And your quaint ol' southern state views.

Uncle Sam, dear Sammy,
You avuncular rogue.
Please return us our bat and our ball.
May we have our toy ships
         and our fish and our chips
And our autumn, when you have your fall?

The Daily Page

When I was young I met a sage,
Who warned me about the daily page
And how the items of daily news
Were interlaced with the paper's views.

He explained to me how hyperbole
Was not so very hard to see
And where a headline big and bold
Denied in fact, the story told.

My sage showed how clear minds reject
Rhetoric that would our brains infect
With page on page of celebrity boredom
And those awful ads. – ad nauseam.

The heaviest cross we have to bear
Is the secret news which isn't there.
Hear the crash of silence fall
Upon the news not there at all.

The sage he shared a final thought:
In the newspaper which you bought
The editor's politics, which he wrote
Will decide which way you vote.

Christmas Bonus

A thing of joy, a just reward,
To supplement the pension
Of all our old long serving folk
Without favour or pretension.

It was all of forty years ago,
Ted Heath, (for it was he)
Decreed ten pounds at Christmas time
For every OAP.

The bonus then was ample
For a Christmas spread in style.
Today it has shrunk to an insult
From conmen in denial.

Meanwhile, mega bonuses get paid
To bankers who don't need them,
Who sneer upon the throng and say:
"It's our job to bleed them."

We live in the Land of Bonuses,
Where jolly bankers frisk,
Where we privatise the profit
And nationalise the risk".

Trade Surplus

Show me a butcher with nothing to eat,
There in his shop with all that meat.
What painter of houses, sinner or saint
Can't help himself to a can of paint?
Are electricians, fit and able
Ever in need of wire or cable?
Is the peckish baker's soul so dead
As to miss the chance of fresh baked bread?
How many farmers glad to be born,
Starve through lack of carrots or corn?
And newsagents, people with various views,
Why would they pay to read the news?
So with bankers, their outlook sunny,
Never go short in the House of Money.

Democracy

Of the People
Who in stately mansions dwell
And walk in privilege all their days
Despising those with sweat to sell.

By the People
Who turn the wheels of justice slowly
And throw their statutes in the faces
Of the poor and lowly.

For the People
Of the safe establishment
Who never want for anything,
Save pity for the discontent.

The Pigsty

Ah that's better! The Year of the Pig
Now we can make it really big
Snout in the trough
Slurp up the scoff
Choke on your virtue, we don't give a fig.

Speed

Too slow the pace of evolution
For the Industrial Revolution.
Coal burned to provide the power
Borne by barge at three miles an hour.

In this age of angst and greed
The call comes for much more speed.
HS2 with the elite in it
Burns billions at three miles a minute.

Grabbing Gary

T'was the night before Christmas, with his greedy thoughts rife
Grasping, grabbing Gary wanted the time of his life.
A Christmas Eve party had been planned in advance,
Opportunity for grabbing stood a good chance.

He saw himself gorging on the finest of foods
With liberal libations of all kinds of booze.
He would grab all the limelight – the selfish fellow!
His bearing so assured, so smug and so mellow.

As chair of churchwardens two-man committee
He held plebs in contempt compounded with pity.
At their last AGM as honest folk will tell
He almost grabbed the secretary's job as well.

It had started at playschool with little girls and boys,
Knocking them over and breaking their toys.
Girls did not like him because he spoilt their games,
He kept pulling their hair and calling them names.

Gary was an impetuous insufferable man
Where all must conform to his flimsiest plan.
He was known for his temper and foaming mouth.
The consummate rotter in the north and the south.

He hoped at the party to see Marie-Claire
With her outstanding assets and flaming red hair.
His heart rate shot skywards when she strode through the door
While his eyes stripped her bare of the clothes that she wore.

His flabby hands were twitching with longing and lust
And his brain went awol when he lunged at her bust.
Her reaction was rapid and froze his lewd grin
With her boot to his crutch and her fist to his chin.

Gary writhed on the floor and the band stopped playing.
The mass media combined to give him a flaying.
Gary grabbed the headlines; now we knew him too well,
T'was the night before Christmas and he was in Hell.

Interglobalisation (or Move Over Rover)

Green, green men from the Planet Mars
Float down to feed on Cadbury bars.
Easy to please
They smell no cheese,
Or miss the tasty homemade cars.

Advice For Chancellor

We know that jobs are in jeopardy
And growth is somewhat tardy,
While roses still bloom in Picardie
And poplars grow tall in Lombardy.

We hear you're a touch foolhardy,
(Some say downright mardy.)
Your colleagues fat and lardy,
And Etonian tories lahdi-dahdi.

So blooming well grow the economy
From Lombard Street in the populous City,
Prune the roses in Picardie,
Cut branches off the Bank of Lombardy
And repatriate the jobs from Jeopardy.
You see young Georgie, it's easy-peasy!

Conference Season

Political party conferences
Are, as a general rule,
Held in highly salubrious places
Like Brighton, Bournemouth and Blackpool.

Once embedded in plush hotels
Panting, full of fervour
Delegates, up bright eyed for the jolly
Seek something they might savour.

The powerful party hierarchies
Mouthe perfect orations,
Which can sway the feeble minded
And earn standing ovations.

Does any of this matter? The posing,
Empty pledges? Whips at Westminster!
Real power, as you know, is brokered
Somewhere more sinister.

As on luxury yachts, at cocktail parties,
In country houses, at the races,
In Beijing, Berlin, boardrooms, park benches
And less salubrious places.

"Oh Dear"

Outside Bangor

It was in a motel just outside Bangor
When first I met my Doppelganger.
His eyes were watery and lips tinged blue
He minded me of one I knew.

Whither goest thou said I?
He'd furrowed brow and reddened eye.
You know where, said he quietly aside
And deep within me something died.

We've travelled together this rocky road
Shared the burden – bourn the load,
We know the end and see its' coming.
Cold tears from his eyes are running.

So we part the while and say farewell,
No more on thoughts of sadness dwell,
But raise our eyes beyond the hill
Where all is peace and all is still.

Wistful Smiles

Safely buried they cleared out Granddad's shed
And dusted round the corners of his life,
Remembered laughing when Grandma said
How lucky she had been to be his wife.
They tied labels on his wasted daydreams
Filed his fantasies in a biscuit tin.
Bundled up odd thoughts, vague visions in reams
And put them with his musings in the bin:

There along his path of broken pavements
Threading between the kerbs of duty miles
Turned away his face from happy moments
Taught himself to savour wistful smiles.
Wind blown hymns, sad prayers, found it futile
Exchanging tears for one last wistful smile.

Oh Dear

A very shy lad from Ryde
Paid cash for a Malaysian bride,
But he let out a cry
When they sent him a Thai
And went from Ryde to Hyde.

A Poet's Prayer

Save me oh Lord, I fervently pray,
From the fell clutch of the deadly cliché
And if as a poet I am ever to function,
Stop me starting off with a conjunction.

Rack me, put me on eternal damnation
If I don't cut down on alliteration.
Punish my puns with rigour and zest
And ignore my limp plea "I gave of my best".
Please cut me some slack regarding analogy,
Just find me a slot in an anthology.

Endow me with talent and vision so pure
That my poems will delight, inspire and endure.
May I write as I please – perhaps rant and rail?
And, with your protection, stay out of jail?

"Big Fat Breakfast?"

Nothing Makes Sense

It was very many years ago
And wearing woad were we,
When Eastern scribes and mystics
Were pondering numeracy.

They could not help but notice
Assistance with their plans,
Their very own ten digits
Appended to their hands.

At a time before computers –
Not yet the abacus,
When fingers must in union cried:
"You can count on us".

Symbols named and values given.
One genius became a hero,
While others strived, he contrived
To invent the number zero.

It is nothing in itself,
Having no obvious worth.
Also known as nix, nil and zilch
And oh, and 'nowt' up north.

So let us raise a glass to nothing.
'Tis the nought which earns our thanks
For making a pound worth ten time more
In our little piggy banks.

Silk and Iron

Hickory hammer handles
hold heavy hammer heads,
Where the finest sewing needles
guide the finest silken threads.

So off lad to your anvil
To learn Life's Iron Rules:
You only get out what you put in
And no-one suffers fools.

Befriend your frame young lady,
Choose your thread with care.
Weave your thoughts into pictures caught
In the sunlight of your hair.

Then at the end your best accounts
May pass the sternest test,
And the small voice within will know
If you gave of your best.

Bank Holiday

Shouldn't you be joining the M6 tailback,
Or up Snowdon with a ninety pound pack?
They say Luton Airport's the place to be
Along with the rest of humanity.
And bunjee jumping performed in the buff
Is exciting, pulsating, 'Boy's Own' stuff.
You could try shin-kicking on Ilkley Moor,
Though it can leave the shanks decidedly sore!

But there you sit, alone in your garden,
Obviously happy – beg your pardon.
You were there last week and the months before
You toil and you rest and your spirits soar.
Quietly peaceful, blending with nature
Garnering wisdom, becoming mature.

Pulling The Lion's Tail

Britannia ruled the seven seas,
Fishing filled our freezers.
Cod war breaks out, relations freeze,
Fingers point at Geysers.

Financial meltdown bankrupts banks,
Landsbanki paid top rates,
Yet frozen savings earn no thanks
For Geysers and their mates.

Volcanic fall-out darkens skies,
The Geysers strike again!
See the spirit of Iceland rise,
So cool, but what a pain.

Words

Long words, short words, hard to sort words,
Harsh words, kind words, hard to find words,
Learnt words, taught words, sold words, bought words,
Written words, spoken words, grave words, silly words.

Words of peace, words of war,
Words you haven't heard before.
Words of love, words of spite,
Words you thought best not to write.

Uttered words, muttered words,
Stuttered words and buttered words,
Misspelled words, the mispronounced
Some off the tongue come unannounced.

Words evolved for communication
Words expect reciprocation.
Words can bond sister and brother,
Families, neighbours, one another.

Words unite and yet divide,
Text and script, groom and bride.
The word, will always be, the word,
Forever sharper than the sword.

My Word!

The Professor D.Lit. awoke in a daze
Scattering words and clauses in wonderouse ways,
Confused about syntax
Forgot to pay road tax
Had his sentence reduced to a phrase.

All In All

Paradoxical man,
What is his name?
Each one unique,
Yet all the same.

Forged in fire
Cooled in ice,
Man evolved,
Found his voice.

Sits astride all
Time and space,
God is all
The human race.

Or, but a speck
Of cosmic dust?
Believe it true,
If you must.

Paradoxical man,
God's guessing game,
All unique, and
All the same.

Matron

You may not see her, she's working free
Tho' she keeps in touch with our G.P.
The old, the poor, those in distress,
She's a vital part of the N.H.S.

Aching joints, eyesight on the blink,
Short term memory out of sync,
But Matron's here, she calms our nerves.
What soothing cups of tea she serves!

Matron makes sure we take our pills,
Matron helps us make our wills.
Down the stairs she guides our feet,
Ditto down the busy street.

Matron's with us each step we go,
Big fat breakfast? No, no, no!
She wears no frumpy uniform,
Or chases lads from the nurses dorm.

She's feisty, full of humanity,
Served her time in Holby City.
Accidents are her speciality -
Did twenty years in Casualty.

You will not see her standing there,
Or sitting in the kitchen chair,
Nor fretting about unmade beds.
Dear Matron lives, inside our heads.

Robert Robot

Computers became that much quicker
Did a slicker, cheaper job.
Out with heart, in with ticker,
Man got smarter, created Bob.
Not just smart but idle too,
Realised late he'd blown it,
In a world no longer new
And far too late to own it:

Human progress should not be curbed
Nuclear waste gains sov'reignty.
Let fossil fuels lie undisturbed,
There's energy a-plenty.
Renewables wax abundant
And Bob considers Man redundant.

"When Man Culls Man"

Peace Postponed

The citizens of Belgrade
Came bearing gifts of wood.
We named our theatre after them,
It was fitting that we should.

Two cities twinned together –
Peace pledged for evermore.
A bond of brotherhood united
By some eternal law.

Then up spake General Jingo:
"Release the dogs of war"
And so the Belgrade's timber
Was stained with Serbia's gore.

Peace Poem Oct 2003

H.M.S. Peace

End of Empire, more admirals than ships
Pipe him ashore to his fine country seat
Peace is the word on everyone's lips.

Farewell Navy and the mast he worships
Westering warrior's mission complete
End of Empire, more admirals than ships.

Cruel axe from the oak England's heart rips
Blood running gundecks drain England's heart beat
Peace is the word on everyone's lips.

Grey wolf-of-the-sea through misty strait slips
To a silent dockyard's rusty retreat
End of Empire, more admirals than ships.

Bring on the croquet and quoits amidships
Converted corvettes with cabins en-suite
Peace is the word on everyone's lips.

'Cruisers a cruising' the old captain quips
Our fairwind future unfurls a clean sheet
End of empire, more admirals than ships
Peace is the word on everyone's lips.

Moments When

When baby first said 'Mamma',
When baby first said 'Dadda'.
When brother Tommy banged his drum
In the most outrageous manner.

When fortune smiled and the sun shone,
When steps were light and future bright.
When flocks of sparrows filled the air.
When both mum and dad were there.

When daddy wore a manly beard.
When baby's first tooth appeared.
When mummy brushed his curly hair,
When spring sprung and all was fair.

When Tommy found himself a job
And earned a wage of thirty bob.
When Tommy wooed and wed a lass,
When work slows and his woes amass.

When Tommy skint did soon enlist,
When he showed the Hun an iron fist.
When he had a gun and clean socks,
When he came home in a wooden box.

Give Peace A Chance

Remember well his words of importance,
Enshrined in the music of Liverpool:
All we are saying is give peace a chance.

He brought to this world love in abundance,
His lessons for us were not learnt at school.
Remember well his words of importance.

Imagine lacking peace and tolerance,
When man culls man he becomes his own ghoul.
All we are saying is give peace a chance.

Behind war lies the dead hand of finance,
From the moneymen's mouths rich juices drool.
Remember well his words of importance.

The sidewalk saw John's final appearance,
Slain on the street by the warmonger's tool.
All he was saying is give peace a chance.

John Lennon Airport marks his acceptance
In love from the people of Liverpool.
Remember well his words of importance –
All we are saying is give peace a chance.

Alliance

Cowboy President, whistling Yankee Doodle.
Hey yo dogsbody, help me win this war,
Boy next door Brit Pop, pretty nodding poodle.

The plot's a peach, our enemies feudal
Ordnance positioned for shock and awe
Cowboy President, whistling Yankee Doodle.

Rusty Iron Lady, too old to canoodle
Lappy dog, happy dog, lies on her floor
Boy next door Brit Pop, pretty nodding poodle.

I'm your whipper-in, this is no flap doodle
Through their rag-tag ranks our crusaders pour
Cowboy President, whistling Yankee Doodle.

Sterling's on the slide, less shine than the rouble
Buys blood on the sand and oil from the bore.
Boy next door Brit Pop, pretty nodding poodle.

 Listen up limey, we can make big boodle,
Don't worry about finer points of law.
Cowboy President, whistling Yankee Doodle,
Boy next door Brit Pop, pretty nodding poodle.

Boudicca

The Romans brought us plumbing
And roads so straight and true.
They also brought their iron heel
And told us what to do.

Boudicca was a patriot,
Her veins coursed British blood.
Her feet stood firm on British soil
And she knew where she stood.

Boudicca was a terrorist
And carried a fiery brand.
She led her tribe in harassment
Scorching Romans from our land.

One day the soldiers took her
And flogged her flesh full sore,
Giving our brave insurgents
Good cause to hate them more.

Back to rotting Rome the proud legions slunk,
Their empire finally fell apart.
Heroic Boudicca our rebel Queen remains,
Close by the nation's heart.

Juvenile Delinquent

Adolf was a loutish lad
Knew all about Reich pudding,
How puerile strode his jackboots,
Durch alle Strasse thudding.

Extermination

Recently, on TV, we saw the Nuremberg trials,
Nazi vermin like caged rats
Issuing fierce denials.
Shown the horror of Belsen –
Utter abomination,
Saw no hope, when they smelt the rope
Of their own extermination.

Poppies

The poppy blows o'er Flanders
Where many a brave soldier fell.
The blood soaked soil remembers
A tragic tale to tell.

Many a mother heartbroken,
Many a wife distraught.
Wild poppies followed the slaughter
To a peace so dearly bought.

Politicians promised eternal peace,
Though history shows the lie.
Poppies promise hope and joy,
But men are born to die.

The sound of guns moves eastwards
We would tame the Taliban.
Now record crops of poppies thrive
In old Afghanistan.

The white and purple flowers
Of Papaver Somniferum
Mask a poison payload
We know as opium.

And it's heading straight for Blighty
To hit our towns and cities.
Why, oh why, should it be so?
For sure, a million pities.

When will we begin to see
The folly of our ways
And beat our swords to ploughshares
In peace to live our days?

Scant Booty

On soles sewn in Northamptonshire
They trudged through Flanders mud
And Grief had watched their souls expire
As they gave up their blood.

On a blasted shell-shocked battlefield
Our booted heroes lay.
Death before his altar kneeled,
Foreclosed the light of day.

Brave colliers too in leather shod
Descended pits of doom.
Brothers through dark galleries trod
Deep down the daily tomb.

The war to end wars proved a myth,
The Bosch belay the gate.
Lace up your hob-nails Private Smith
We march towards our fate.

Victory's dug for, so we live
To dig again at leisure.
Our army boots have more to give,
But History will not treasure.

And still sons die and mothers rue,
Why are we so unkind?
What feeds those maggots squirming through
The eyelets of the blind?

Out Of The Darkness

Deep beneath the sun scorched Arabian sand
Lay a sunless unctuous carbonised lake.
With my fellow atoms our close set band
Were meant to lie forever unawake.
From above the crusading drill burst through
Through the darkness a circle of azure,
At once our world was ended and we knew
All peace had gone, all certainty unsure:

Thus torn from our cosy primeval bed
To transportation and refinery.
Now under the boot of a petrol head
Combustion, exhaustion and misery.
But the Fates fell fickle and Time can lag
Found me integral with a plastic bag.

Vladimir

The TV baker's cake looks sad.
Did he put the fruit in?
Maybe he did, maybe he didn't.
Best blame Vladi Putin!

The weather lets us down again,
Clouds cross skies a-scootin'.
Cold air stream from Siberia comes –
Must be Vladi Putin!

Gardeners in a right old strop,
Plants so slow at rootin'.
Blame the garden centre, and yes,
Blame that Vladi Putin!

Fallible flautist dropped some notes,
Lost his place when tootin'.
The whole ballet thing got him down
So blames Vladi Putin!

Warless warriors want a scrap,
Time to start disputin'.
Need a decoy to take the rap –
Why not Vladi Putin?

Printed in Great Britain
by Amazon

79476296R00098